Esse

A book of Poetry and Illustrations

Roshani Gash

Illustrations by Pavitra Svana

Roshani Gash & Pavitra Ivana

Esse

Esse Copyright © 2020 by Roshani Gash and Pavitra Svana. All Rights Reserved.

No part of this book may be reproduced in any form or by any electronic or mechanical means including information storage and retrieval systems, without permission in writing from the author and illustrator. The only exception is by a reviewer, who may quote short excerpts in a review.

Cover designed by Pavitra Svana.

This book is a work of non-fiction. No characters have been invented or names used. It consists of original poetry and illustrations inspired by the insights of the authors.

ISBN – 9798640241181
First Printing: May 2020
Place of Publication – United States of America

Roshani Gash & Pavitra Svana

This book is dedicated to the beautiful sisterhood we share, and to artists all around the world.

Preface

All the works in this book are originals. All poetry in this book is written by Roshani Gash and all illustrations are done by Pavitra Svana.

The cover of this book is also designed by Pavitra Svana. The poetic interpretation below conveys one of the deeper meanings behind this piece, to shine light on the intricacies of human connections and to know that ultimately, we all truly are one.

Walking alone, though not in reality,
As many lives walk alongside of me,
Unknown strangers in parallel invisible lanes,
Paving paths with so much similarity;

As life goes on, faces change constantly,
Newer companions enter seamlessly,
Every face etches into new memories,
Though many fade away by losing touch entirely;

But I do feel our stories are connected truly,
For taking the same turns in moments simultaneously,
Making us closer in spirit though they are strangers to me,
For all stories are connected, surely one day we'll see.

~ R.G.S

The world needs more reasons to come together rather than grow further apart and we hope this book can be one of the ways to accomplish this simple thought and wish through art.

Contents

Writer 13

Storm 15

Ache 16

Entwined 19

Perfectly incomplete 21

Hope 23

Today 24

Yearning 27

Fort 29

The standing man 31

Save my soul 33

Wordless 35

Warcry 37

Betrayal 39

The clearing 41

Wandering souls 43

Empathy 45

Touching moment	47
Fearless farewell	49
Self	51
Run of the mill	53
Soul catcher	55
Lost soul	57
Hereditary	59
True lies	61
Symphony of Synapse	63
Moment of truth	65
Masks	67
Refugee	69
Flipsides	71
The Maker	74
Umbilical Cord	77
Free	79
Snow	81
Lock and Key	83

Esse

"*V*eracious essence of me, which comes naturally"

Roshani Gash & Pavitra Svana

Writer

I write because it flows through me,
Like the trickling sea it runs free,
I write to share what might set free,
Your secrets or notions playing hide and seek;

I write to speak in my language of serenity,
To tell you that you hold so much beauty,
I write to be who I know is truly me,
And to show you the world that I see;

Because when there is no time to see,
What truly lies inside your psyche,
You are losing all that you can be,
And the chance to fulfill your destiny;

The restlessness will refuse to flee,
But in it there is some comfort to seek,
To build what fulfills your entirety,
In this one shot at life, this is the key.

Storm

There is a silent storm stirring away,
It has enveloped me and you,
Within its heart there is no disarray,
Just a stillness strong and true;
Something in you gives me the ray,
That there is no reason to be blue,
To weather the storm together today,
And come out stronger too;
In your kind eyes I am lost, and I fray,
Knowing that you will piece me together anew,
So, I crumble and flow like breeze over the brae,
Like water that flows till stillness comes through,
But some things cannot be tamed they say,
The way I am the storm now and so are you.

Ache

I cannot remember how I got here,
The last book you read, I am holding close to me,
I have been drifting, scattered like debris,
I am the broken fragments of you and me;

Here I stand, but an inch from icy waters,
Just minutes from being able to see,
The you I lost, the you that wanders,
The you that once lived inside my psyche;

My tears are dry, my mind now ponders,
My feet now burn submerged in the sea,
I cannot feel any other emotions,
But the fierce ache in my heart that has silenced the banshee;

Esse

They say time does matter and time always heals,
But time for me is a long road of misery,
With the ache so numbing, time only reveals,
There isn't now and never will be a remedy;
The book in my hand now floats on the waves,
And the trace of a rose it did once hold shines at me,
Though the rose is gone, its essence left behind,
As evidence of existence in another entity;
I feel my soul breathe inside,
Like a lightning hit, you come alive in front of me,
Enlightening the traces of you that remains in my heart,
And as long as I breathe, you will live in me.

Roshani Gash & Pavitra Ivana

Entwined

Your scrutinizing eyes looking on,
Deducing perceptions of what you see,
Is undisputed truth exposed?
Or is there ambiguity?

Frail and weak, living in dormancy,
The future looks bleak, constantly,
Turning our backs on each other Inadvertently,
Failing to see eye to eye any longer, in this journey;

Entwined in this worldly unity,
While deeply disconnected are we,
Suspended in a state of unconsciousness,
With no point of return in visibility;

In the deep realms of our reality,
Feeding on what is left, comes misery,
Lashing out, adding to the pain ruthlessly,
Our demeanor breaks and emotions ooze free;

How long can one live on?
For the sake of all, but who should count,
What stops us and never allows,
To make this call and let the chips fall.

Perfectly incomplete

There is a hole in my heart,
That no-one can fill,
Was it there from the start?
And just sitting still?

Perhaps a dart after dart,
Revealed that now I'm ill,
Through my life that I chart,
Choices made by my will;

Some heal some tear apart,
And some that just drill,
This evolving hole in my heart,
That I've embraced with skill;

Acknowledging weakness is an art,
I'm neither shackled nor my pain nil,
The truth, you can't always outsmart,
Sometimes it is okay to feel the chill,
I grow after coming apart,
And carry it with me all the way uphill.

Hope

My eyes register a stunning display,
A silent sheet of silver and grey,
I stare without blinking or breathing I daresay,
In this motionless moment I just want to stay;
But life isn't perfect, there is always disarray,
There is no place for fear or dismay,
So, I pick up a little pebble and throw it away,
Off into the water I watch it splash and splay;
The ripples move beautifully across the bay,
Eventually pausing, no longer does the water sway,
The calm returns once again to convey,
That everything in time will turn out okay.

Today

If you know what to look for,
Your every question has a key;

If you know what to listen for,
Truth will be whispered to set you free;

If you know what choices were meant for,
You will know how rights and wrongs shaped history;

If you know what people come together for,
In love you'll find pure divinity;

If you never question what you're looking for;
You'll never recognize your destiny;

And all the magic your life is meant for,
Will be lost in your ignorant futility;

Why fret, what are you waiting for,
Your only control is in today's reality.

Roshani Gash & Pavitra Ivana

Esse

Yearning

In the flash of a second you were gone,
I know you see my endlessly breaking heart,
Every day and every night the longing lives on,
For a moment or reflection of us together not apart;

Through any door walk in or my name call on,
Somehow, I believe you will waltz in for a new start,
But in my weakest of moments, I know you are gone,
Though the hope, O! the hope is all I have now sweetheart;

To arrested memories of you in every mirror I'm drawn,
The reflections of your arms around me is a work of art,
I blatantly choose this way to see you living on,
Because in moments of truth I'm alone as you did depart;

People tell me I cannot cease to move on,
And that living in our virtual togetherness is not smart,
But your presence in nothingness cannot be a con,
Yet no sign of you in my reality hurts like a dart;

I know it is life not death you'd want me to dwell on,
I know exactly what in me you still do impart,
And you'd tell me to make way for a new dawn,
Find courage for new journeys to chart;

I know I want with peace for you to move on,
When from my ache and selfishness I can break apart,
So, I'll try to turn a brick around every day here on,
Each time I'll stand again after millions of times I fall apart.

Fort

Back again behind these walls I live now,
None can enter nor can their shadows crawl,
A dark but safe haven for me somehow,
Once again, I have nothing more to give at all,

To my sacred truth I surrender and bow,
Here is where I can crumble and fall,
No fallacies, no sound of another broken vow,
Only my memory you will be able to recall,

Only with myself is there trust in a powwow,
I am a beating heart not a fantasy to enthrall,
Tears are too real for you so I'm bidding you ciao,
Do not bother to try, I am now immune to your call,

I will reassemble piece by piece anyhow,
Without you, my yet another downfall,
Take every piece of you away right here and now,
I will heal again quietly behind my protective wall.

The standing man

I am stopped in my steps as I feel a subtle chill,
An illusion of time stopping at his will,
There is stillness in the air that surrounds him,
None do stop but I'm lost in the whim;
The day goes by and I forget him until,
I see he hasn't moved and maybe never will,
I look around me and no one else can see his thrill,
I take a step forward, surrendering to my free will;
Frozen eyes seem to have nothing to spill,
Set in stone is his form for he's standing stock-still,
Unswerving, he just stands until the light goes dim,
In the blink of an eye there's but a shadow left of him.

Roshani Gash & Pavitra Ivana

Save my soul

When far too much damage is done,
And rock bottom is my seventh heaven,
Lying blank on splayed facts unhidden,
Nowhere in sight is my point of return;
Inner strength flinches, overridden,
Weakness seeps through, no longer forbidden,
Unravelling in its wake such venom,
Leaving me savagely guilt stricken;
Wicking scraps of peace from within,
Desolate, a recluse I have become,
Witnessing griefs of a life I succumb,
Sinking further from the light of the burning sun;
Broken soul, can one ever mend?
With novel thoughts, what can I fare?
Can a dying whisper of hope bravely stare?

Into my shambles, alluring me to repair;
All that I have lost, though I cannot reclaim,
But my frame of mind, I try to tame,
Vandalizing the debris that lies,
Of a shackled soul, that no longer chides;
In an ounce of will, I willingly confide,
Letting all my regrets be put aside,
Liberated, taking in my stride,
The tender soul with heed I guide;
As years will go by, one day I will cast aside,
To revel in the glory of just having tried and tried,
A once exempted soul, will then blissfully reside,
In the shimmering light of a blessed life's delights.

Wordless

Teardrops frozen in the pages of a book,
Words made illegible by those dews,
Released in them I found someone's blues,
Laying on a library shelf in the middle of a room;

A memory once imparted,
Does now visibly loom,
Was it a cry of relief?
Or was it heartbreaking gloom?

None of it could have mattered,
Though with questions my mind was consumed,
Of a piece in the past of I knew not whom,
Yet I found myself lost and I just couldn't be immune;

As I stood there in stark silence,
Staring baffled yet in tune,
With emotions within me,
That without a word a book had strewn.

Warcry

A cannon war has been struck,
With bombardments and a blazing fire,
Hit by the wave of unfortunate luck,
Lay remnants of a broken empire;
No shelter, no food, not a buck,
Fending in situations so dire,
Lives tainted by those running amuck,
Leaving survival their only desire;
Ones who are by power awestruck,
Turn blind to countless soul shaking pyres,
History so chilling now so writ,
In generations to come, only pain will transpire.

Roshani Gash & Pavitra Svana

Betrayal

Blanched in disappointments and lies,
Soaking velvet the fabric of our troth,
A soundless moment of despair strikes,
Breaking what remained of our ties;

Drowned in ignorance, deceit blindsides,
The core of credence so built with might,
Your perfidious token now lunges inside,
But my fateful crumble just seems to ignite,
The light that unmasks the truth of us both;

All that is left of you is now wedged in my spine,
Revoking all emotions and devotions alike,
Embracing the pain that now quenches my fright,
Stronger I revive, once shaken, I now stand upright;

Reality shall strike to disillusion your psych,
You may realize it is me you have lost in hindsight,
Dismissed are those virtues that are virtual and trite,
My faithless friend turned foe is now erased from sight.

The clearing

Ten planks of wood over this water stream,
Where once you and I together had been,
Though you wait on the other side to reconvene,
Your restlessness is so palpable, hopeless you seem;

Somehow, I remain suspended in this scene,
As impaling memories return unforeseen,
My eyes fight to look past the smoke screen,
But I see the larger distances lingering in between;

You take the first step forward, with all of your mein,
To give us another chance, hoping to redeem,
My self-preservation comes reflexively to intervene,
This in my eyes I know you have seen;

Though you do not convey, all I hear is your silent scream,
I turn around, walk away, feeling we are just a pipe dream,
Perhaps tomorrow in our try love will reign supreme,
But for now, only in my seclusion am I serene.

Wandering souls

Aimlessly wandering souls.
Seldom do ask what are their roles,
Watching midnight passerby's strolls,
Not really on opposite ends of the poles;

Perhaps filling away some holes,
Far away from past and all its trolls,
Never held back by unanswered goals,
Incomplete today, perhaps tomorrow's wholes;

After smoky nights and ashtray filled bowls,
New day creeps in, once again the dice rolls,
Moment by moment is the only way future unfolds,
The only way to be for lost souls;

All the rules made by generic polls,
Don't hold true, they are free from controls,
Connecting dots amongst stars and floors,
I am now and forever one of these wandering souls.

Empathy

A life lived consciously,

Lasts in hearts eternally,

For stamps of yourself you impart unconsciously,

In lives touched by you even momentarily,

I wonder how one does choose to be,

Living moments of dreams and reality,

Do the hardships define?

Or is it fractions of sanity?

That makes us the people we want to be,

Though many may melt your heart,

Ones who win it come by rarely,

So, here is a toast to generosity,

And hope that in life you choose wisely,

To bring from darkness to light human sanctity,

And make life beautiful for all those in your vicinity.

Roshani Gash & Pavitra Ivana

Touching moment

Hold on sweet love, you say,
Convinced you can make it go away,
Squeezing tighter, sand keeps slipping away,
From fingers of your hands in mine;

Frozen love and tears flash both ways,
Until something greater paves through to sleigh,
What could have lead us astray?
From fervid immortal unspoken desires;

But lost are words in this display,
Of healing pain that can only last today,
Bereft and void such a loss may weigh,
When the memories of you will be forever in replay;

Every second I give more of me away,
Till my last drop of ardor comes your way,
I watch the last of you slipping away,
Let go now sweet love, is all I can say.

Fearless farewell

In this one last twirl let me stay enthralled,
And make this split second last above all,
Merging through perfect oblivion,
We recklessly wish to forestall;

The crumble of our tangible fantasy,
That will inevitably lead to a curtain call,
Beautiful can blissful ignorance be,
But it will disappear once and for all;

In the blink of our intoxicated eyes,
Our grim realities shall befall,
I will be forced to make peace all in all,
That it never was meant for the long haul;

Acceptance will inadvertently begin to crawl,
And our vacant lives will resume from this stall,
Though in moments of my heart's sincerity,
Our last dance I will fondly recall;

And the pain of losing what could have been,
I will learn to relinquish, and heal from my fall,
Somethings in life are not meant to be,
Though its fragile dream does live on,
But no good can come clinging to memories,
So, forgive the possibilities of you and me,
Such loving hearts can never be forlorn.

Self

Cold splash of water to awaken my drowsy pace,
Feels like broken shards of glass trickling down my face,
Wakeful eyes habitually blanket disorders,
Prevailing ignorance aiding in this reassurance;
Walking barefoot I look around,
Desperate to hear footsteps but there isn't a sound,
I wait by the window till after sundown,
Continuing the journey to make right his every wrong;
Flashes of lightning make way for a storm,
A flicker that unveils me that I cannot decline,
Watching my bloodless reflection undaunted,
Displaying honest emotions unconsciously veiled for so long;

Washing unfilled wishes rain starts pouring down,
Releasing my seclusions, I am unwearied and strong,
Grateful and blessed my intuitions are awake,
For once I am glad, my mirror can no longer fake;
No words of wisdom addressed to me,
Ever allowed me to embrace,
What I had to learn through self-discovery,
In this reflection of hopeless faith,
Now with truth no longer hidden,
I refuse to live in someone else's disgrace.

Run of the mill

Is it not surprising?
In those freeing moments of clarity,
How we each have somehow come to be,
Easily convinced into a life of repeatability;
Generations pass on viability,
And life is tailored with responsibilities,
Striving for success with credibility,
Ignorantly losing one's true identity;
Our purpose on earth takes a backseat,
In pointless pursuits our passions lay asleep,
Avoiding steering away from our creed,
In truth, we are fearful of being freed.

Roshani Gash & Pavitra Svana

Soul catcher

Drifting in the darkness, light years away,
A silhouette soaks energy, floats soundlessly,
Draped and cloaked in shadows of loss,
With such grace and so very enchantingly,
She hovers around bewitchingly;

Pure drops of floating lights,
Fall through darkness swiftly,
For a moment splaying their bright light,
They merge into the dark creature's anatomy;

Snatched within seconds so swiftly,
Under the cloak of this being, discreetly,
The reaper breathes in the new lights,
To continue her lifeless existence eternally;

Blazed in the fiery memories,
Of the souls now lost entirely,
The catcher of souls, trembles momentarily;

Till all is lost in this black hole of a being,
In a world so upside down,
In all aspects, defying vitality,
Surrendered are souls in this beyond,
Caught in dark realms of the reaper's caprice.

Lost soul

Standing on the edge of a world beneath,
Letting everything slip from underneath my feet,
Floating in the intoxicating whirlwind,
Nowhere to go, no will to think;

With no sense of space or time within,
Losing control of all sadness I sink,
Only to find that sense of peace I am missing,
But a moment's escape at the edge of the brink;

Bridge the gap of time with thoughts,
Make each memory you make count,
Sing me the song I missed yesterday,
Take that first step, follow what the instinct does say;

Walking across my life and dreams,
Love is ageless like it was promised, it beams,
Pulling me back from numbness unseen,
Drowning my pain, a new world takes me in.

Hereditary

I am inaudible but do not be mistaken,
For my thoughts race rapidly,
You are quiet but I see through it,
As now you stand in front of me;

A bitter truth to which I am defiant,
For I fear thinking it quite admittedly,
You are my mirror and I am frightened,
I have become who you once were to me;

I live in pain with this shattering tragedy,
When this side of you possesses my entirety,
I become someone unrecognizable,
Carrying this cloak of raging misery;

I stayed silent in fear of hurting you,
But with you gone that fear still lingers true,
I try and let go of all the things I know,
All the things you put a child through;

And now the evil rage masks my sanity,
In dark moments though this filter I see,
The paranoia takes over instinctively,
To inflict the pain before anyone can touch me;

I stand before you in want of being free,
With forgiveness in my heart, a gift to me,
I want to be rid of all the agony,
To change my future as I now foresee,
With hope in my heart and tenacity.

True lies

It all comes down to this,
A secret of sorts, a kiss,
A want of eternal bliss,
But what I never had I cannot miss;
It sometimes boils down to this,
A breath, a silent prose of his,
A fraction, emotion gone amiss,
Something for us to reminisce;
It may never turn into this,
As reality is our fantasy's abyss,
Where all that is left is the rationale's hiss,
And all traces of truth can go remiss.

Roshani Gash & Pavitra Svana

Symphony of Synapse

Deluded, written off I am, still letting myself fall,
Into deeper darkness where confinement is null,
Thoughts keep racing on light rays,
There is no escape I want;

What you see is a disaster,
But I humbly behold,
Mastering directions unforeseen,
My brain silently works through it all;

There's sweet symphony if you cared to hear,
But you arrest your soul,
I am the one in a straitjacket,
Yet it is you whose life is in stall;

I am free floating anywhere I am,
No confinement will withhold,
The journeys I can take each day,
Choosing to lose self-control.

Moment of truth

Dew drops trickle down long lashes,
Soundless shatters of a breaking heart,
Words unspoken scattered everywhere,
A badgered spirit screaming to come out;

Falling sand inside the hourglass,
Watching motionless as time passes by,
Waiting desperately for divine intervention perhaps,
Yet wounds lay open as life goes by;

Quilting faith, barely standing at all,
Clawing inside, crumbling with freight,
Quaking beneath quivering soles of my feet,
Reality begs for recognition outright;

Yet closed are eyes as diamonds drip by,
An emotional release revealing awful insights,
No stopping of soul from crumbling any more,
A frozen moment of truth urging respite.

Masks

Happy or sad, mysterious or mad,
Every emotion he drew with his hands,
A vision he would see, and pour it with glee,
Into this empty mold gently,

Days would go by,
Without tiring he would paint,
Till one day he stopped,
To see what he had made,

And Alas! he was shocked,
To see millions of eyes,
Staring back intently,
With meaningful insights,

Though the masks were different,
To him they were alike,
For every face that he had painted,
Showed all his hidden desires,

Masks do cover the true face,
But not the feelings he would say,
For each person picks a mask,
That is their mirror image,

It may conceal your secrets,
Or might just cover your skin,
But the truth will always lie,
In what lies within!

Esse

Refugee

Escaping to save what is left of me,
Protecting the remnants of my free will solemnly,
Escaping in the darkness as a refugee,
Running far away from all the eyes on me;
Beaten I am not, nor shall I ever be,
Purely in search of rest even momentarily,
For tomorrow it shall begin all over again,
And ready I know I will have to be;
So, do me this kindness, this act unselfishly,
If for nothing else, for the sake of humanity,
let me stay in here, away from evils of the world,
Just for now let me have my share of tranquility,
After sunrise, I promise, you will never see me.

Roshani Gash & Pavitra Svana

Flipsides

Let us play a game together again,
What you choose, you get,
To find your truth, will you dare?
Discover what you have hidden underneath;

Clothed in what is called sanity,
Until your fears start to surface,
Leaving you bare, so you see,
Everything you are capable of;

What you choose and what you can be,
Surprise yourself momentarily,
Revealing raw bits of your personality,
Ones you have tightly ensnared fearfully;

Afraid to stray too far from concepts of reality,
They say the truth shall set you free,
So, will you recognize your entirety?
While the conscience looks on, patiently;

What will you choose and what is your humanity?
Walking on this tightrope unconsciously,
Sometimes pacing forward confidently,
But holding back in moments, as one should be;

Echoes the voice of reason, craving stability,
The flipsides of you look on anxiously,
Showing you, your plausible individualities,
Bringing blur to focus, the concepts of your extremities;

Those you skewed to never envision in constant un-surety,
Dare to find your truth today and free you shall be,
Now that you see so clearly,
Embrace your light and darkness equally,
To know the essence of who you are choosing to be,
As in denial, you only live aimlessly.

Roshani Gash & Pavitra Svana

The Maker

Weaver of dreams is he,
Not the catcher of terror,
Pouring powerful magic to free,
Your secrets, of which he is a sharer;

Sitting under a large oak tree,
He corrects your hidden error,
So, clearer you may always see,
He is your destiny's repairer;

Creating intricate webs to invoke glee,
Skillfully he attaches another feather,
So, all the troubles from your life can flee,
He lives the life of a peace-bearer;

What is built for you, yours it will be,
Working the magic of its seller,
What you don't know, he did foresee,
It is the gift of the dreamcatcher maker.

Roshani Gash & Pavitra Svana

Umbilical Cord

Every link with it bears,
An emotion eternally it wears,
With it, strength immeasurable,
To which nothing compares;

With such authority, you declare,
In all but words your wholehearted care,
Pulses of life are constantly spared,
With luscious love that I revere;

At no time in life am I left unaware,
Of your incredible credence in me,
I find you always near,
Singing my prophesy in my ears;

Engaging faith back in me,
I am forever in your prayers,
And I lean on you so frequently,
Knowing you will always be there;

So, my heart beats in silent gratitude,
To constantly share,
The love brimming in it thanks to you,
With unconditional love and tender care.

Free

Flying and falling papers everywhere,
Sitting back, I watch completely aware,
Words poured out of my being I shared,
Onto those very pages that now float through thin air;

Gambling my sense of peace, I am,
Yet no move I seem to make,
To gather my precious passions,
That only words cared to wear;

Am I frozen in this sense of loss?
Or am I far beyond repair?
Or have the words been laid to rest now?
That I no longer need to bear;

A breath of air fills my lungs just then,
And, a sigh escapes from me unaware,
The hint of a smile plays on my lips gratefully,
As I gather freedom, watching my words escape.

Snow

All colors within me do pour,
I am all shades within my very core,
What you see is my veil so pure,
Like the moonlight on a seashore;

Sunlight melts my every pore,
To set free and restore,
Everything that my white blanket wore,
In winters as the wind sung my lore;

I remain frozen forevermore,
Some detest me, some adore,
But you cannot escape my beauty's allure,
I am peace and it is what I implore.

Roshani Gash & Pavitra Svana

Lock and Key

If you were a snowflake, a unique trove,
I would be the winter all around,
If you were a bright star high above,
I would be the night sky moving into foreground,
If you were a pearl, an oyster's clove,
I would be the ocean bed to which you'd be bound,
If you were the symbol of unity and love,
I would be the hearts in which you'd be found,
If you were the words strung for lyrics thereof,
I would be a melodious symphony's sound,
Whatever we may independently be made of,
Together we build something beautifully profound.

Acknowledgements

This book would have been impossible without the immense support and unconditional love of our family. We are grateful to our parents Shashi and Gaurav and to Pavitra's husband Bhuwan Chandra for always being there and for believing in us even when we fail to believe in ourselves as artists.

Esse

Proseartists

For more collaborative pieces from the authors Roshani Gash and Pavitra Svana please check out their joint Instagram account @proseartists

~ 87 ~

Other books by this author

Snippets: Short Stories

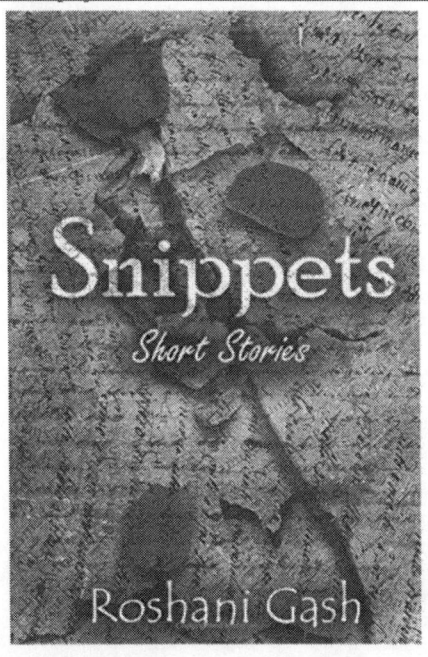

Snippets is a collection of ten short stories by first-time author Roshani Gash. These stories journey through the maze of emotions and relationships whilst capturing the essence of love, loss, happiness, friendship, aspirations, compassion and regrets in one's life. Each story courses through a character's psyche, mapping emotional evolutions like breaking free of one's damaging emotional patterns, whilst also highlighting the passion, peace and beauty one is capable of offering. Above all else, it is about that little bit of magic that one can bring into the world to make it brighter.